WHY IS EVERYBODY LOOKING AT ME

为什么他们都盯着我看？

By
Denis G. Antoine
丹尼斯·安托万

Copyright © 2019 by Denis G. Antoine

ISBN 9781970160055 Ebook
ISBN 9781970160185 Paperback

All rights reserved. No part of this publication may be reproduced, distributed, or transmitted in any form or by any means, including photocopying, recording, or other electronic or mechanical methods without the prior written permission of the publisher. For permission requests, solicit the publisher via the address below through mail or email with the subject line "Attention: Publication Permission".

EC Publishing LLC
11100 SW 93rd Court Road, Suite 10-215
Ocala, Florida 34481-5188, USA

www.ecpublishingllc.com
info@ecpublishingllc.com
+1 (352) 234-6201

Printed in the United States of America

Denis and Tony became good friends when they met in China.

Both men were ambassadors from the Caribbean (Jia le bi). Tony is of Chinese descent and Denis is of African descent.

One day after attending a very important meeting, the ambassadors planned to ride the train to their embassies, located in Beijing, China.

The ambassadors entered a crowded train station and joined the long line of people riding down an escalator to the lower level of the station to board the high speed rail, going from Hangzhou to Beijing.

As the two ambassadors glided slowly down to the platform on the escalator; Ambassador Denis became aware and very startled, when he noticed that so many eyes were watching him.

There were questioning eyes that seem to ask, who this is? Why does he look like that? Where in the world he is from?

Denis begun to look at himself; then he turned to the crowd; and quietly asked Tony who stood close to him.

"Tony, why are they all looking at me?"

Tony smiled and whispered.

"It could be because you look different, being in a crowd among so many with similar looking features."

Denis became self-conscious, but held his chin up, and asked. "Different how?" And he soon began to wave, and smile, and greet any one whose eyes met his.

Many smiles came back, but still he could not fully understand, what was intended by the stares. By the gaze of the crowd, there seem to be curiosity about his presence.

As the Ambassadors boarded the train, Denis reached over to Tony and whispered.

"Tony, my presence seems to disturb the sameness in the appearance of the people in the crowd?"

Tony responded.

"It is very obvious and that's what makes you stand out, it's your pigment Denis."

Now, acting like he was having a visual treat, Denis bowed and made a pleasant expression with his mouth, facing the crowd, he asked.

"Tony, what about my Pigment?"

Tony did not answer.

Denis turned to Tony. "I see beauty in the eyes of all who are looking at me. I hope they see the same looking at me."

Looking over the right shoulder of Denis, someone posed and asked to do a selfie. And to his left, his smile clashed with another, who seemed to be admiring Denis, as if in doubt.

As Denis took his seat on the train, he glanced again across a sea of people, and the entire mass still seemed to be scrutinizing in his direction.

For a while Denis kept looking around and asked himself, wow, they are all still looking at me.

Tony responded. "Denis, are you looking at them, or are they looking at you?"

Denis uttered. "Well, I am sure that you can see that they are not looking at you."

Where we come from, in the Caribbean, we appreciate each other's uniqueness in appearance; and we celebrate that diversity.

People in the Caribbean know each other just the way they are. In Jamaica, the motto is *Out of many one people*; in Trinidad and Tobago, it's *Together we aspire, together we achieve*; and in Grenada, we sing, *As one people one family*. In the family of Caribbean people, there is a wide combination of colors.

"You are so right," said Tony.

"Look at you and me, back home when we meet each other, we just ask 'what's happening brother', or 'what's going on man.'"

In the Caribbean, there is a colorful mix of many skin tones, and features, accepted and embraced. The Caribbean is a welcoming region with rich variety of people; foreign visitors are not distracted because it's a cosmopolitan civilization.

The two Ambassadors sat quietly on the train, but still there were peering eyes examining Denis, again and again.

Denis asked. "Tony, what does it mean? Do you see?"

"Well, Denis, they do not gaze at me, because I look similar."

"Similar!" Denis smiled.

"Yes, I am familiar by my features," said Tony.

"But we are both visitors," reminded Denis.

"Yes," answered Tony. "But in you they just see a foreigner, and they gape because of your hue."

"Tony," Denis jokingly uttered. "But what about your hue? Why don't they scrutinize you?"

Tony laughed. "It's because I look comparable to all, my friend."

"Okay, you look related," Denis remarked. "Is that why their eyes explore me and not you?"

"Yes, yes," said Tony. "But I blend like another brother or neighbor. I do not look like a foreigner in China."

"They may be approving your looks and your expressions; because one black man on a crowded train is not a common sight in China," said Tony.

"So, they are looking at me, because of novelty?" asked Denis.

"Well," said Tony. "I am sure it's because you are the only man of color here and your dark chocolate pigment stands out when all around you have lighter skin."

"Skin tone should not matter. All that should be in our human structures," Denis responded.

"I agree, Denis. With friendship comes understanding, and people meeting people as they travel, awareness makes facial appearance or color disappear."

Denis added. "What counts most today in our world is people's purpose.

Travelers and strangers in China, or anywhere in the world one goes; like smiles, and languages; being different does not mean any one is deficient. With knowledge and sensitivity, skin texture or color should not distract anybody; what makes us alike, should be what makes us more appreciative of each other.

"I agree with you again, Denis," said Tony, while shaking his head.

Denis reacted. "Showing interest and being respectful, when we meet people is the right thing to do; that is why I chuckle, and smile, like I always do when people look at me. I give others permission to smile back at me when I smile."

Tony agreed. "You are right man, and I think it's a show of regard, awe, or they admire, to be invited to take a picture, with a stranger; so, let's show we are both from Jia le bi, and join in the photo with me."

"Tony," Denis remarked. "No fuss, lets meet those questioning eyes always with Caribbean smiles, that we regularly wear."

"I agree with that," Tony acknowledged. "I believe that; because skin tone and texture is not identity, but nature's gift to you and me."

"Yes," Denis nodded. "We need to see each other not for what's different about us, but what's common and for what's unique, and can unite us."

There is so much beauty to be enjoyed from the medley of people's in our universe.

"This experience on the train makes me feel like a child again and I find so much space in me to know more, and still to learn and grow."

"Imagine that there is more than 5000 years of knowledge, and history, in China, and 56 different ethnic composition of faces and yet you see one people," Tony echoed.

"So true and China is still growing," Denis agreed. My feelings of now turn to a grateful joy, for this experience on the high-speed train.

I now connect with those eyes looking at me; and I see the brave countenance of emperors and heroes, majesty of dynasties, and legends of China looking at me.

And as the train pulled into Beijing, Nan Zhan, Denis said to Tony. "Do you see how people move in harmony in Beijing, soon there would be no time to linger about a stranger's appearance. Where they are from or where they are going would mean nothing. People would be accepted as gifts, to one and other, wrapped in multiple colors."

"Yes, man," Denis expressed. "Let's embrace your own colors and all others, with respect. Always remember that our skin wraps us, as common human presents in a kaleidoscope world that reflects us all. Never mind that they are all looking at you."

www.ingramcontent.com/pod-product-compliance
Lightning Source LLC
Chambersburg PA
CBHW071918070526
44583CB00016B/2042